Bank Director

Survival Guide

Bank Director

Survival Guide

By

Charles J Thayer

First Edition

Chartwell Capital Ltd
Palm City, Florida

www.ChartwellCapital.com

ISBN: 978-1973834557

On The Cover

The cover photo is Jimmy Stewart portraying banker George Bailey in the classic movie "It's a Wonderful Life".

In this scene George Bailey passionately describes how his bank serves its customers and benefits their community. His speech restores confidence and his bank "survives" a potential "run" on the bank.

Dedication

"80% of Success is Showing Up"

Woody Allen

Over the past fifty-years my service as a bank executive, board member and/or board advisor has provided me with a wonderful opportunity to work with a great number of outstanding executives and board members.

Most of these relationships were excellent examples of quality management and professional board governance. However, a couple of my board positions and numerous client relationships proved to be extremely challenging and provided invaluable experience for working with troubled management situations and complex board governance issues.

The stories in my previous book, *Credit Check*, describe many of these encounters and provide additional insight on the lessons learned from my mentors.

Survival Guide shares many of the insights and lessons learned from each of these outstanding mentors.

Thank You!

Charles J Thayer

Table of Contents

Preface

"Human beings, who are almost unique in having the ability to learn from the experience of others, are also remarkable for their apparent disinclination to do so."

Douglas Adams
Hitchhiker's Guide to the Galaxy

Survival Guide provides bank directors and bank executives with the tools required to navigate the unique challenges faced by bank board members.

Service as a bank director may have been considered an honor in the past - but times have changed. Today, bank directors assume more personal liability and face greater regulatory requirements than other board positions.

Strong banks are the lifeblood of a healthy, growing community. When you serve as a bank director you have an extraordinary opportunity to contribute to the economic health of your community by helping local businesses grow and create jobs.

Survival Guide provides you with a practical roadmap for making your job as a bank director more effective and rewarding - from the day you join until the day you depart your bank board.

Every board consists of unique talents and personalities so *Survival Guide* is not a "cookbook". Your board and the bank's executive management team need to determine your own "recipe" for success.

Charles J Thayer

Introduction

Survival Guide provides a roadmap to help bank executives and board members function together more effectively. This book does not address compliance with specific regulatory or legal requirements. You should obtain such information from your bank's law firm and bank regulators.

For your protection as a board member it is important that you understand and comply with the business judgment rule, which protects directors by presuming that in making business decisions with regard to the bank, the directors acted on an informed basis, in good faith and in the honest belief that their actions were taken in the best interests of the bank, and not their personal self-interest. However, such protections are not automatic.

To have the protections of the business judgment rule, you as a director are required to act at all times in good faith as to the bank and to observe the key duties of a director: the duties of care and of loyalty. These duties have been developed over many decades by the courts and are articulated in these statements from the Cornell University Law School:

The <u>duty of care</u> stands for the principle that directors and officers of a corporation in making all decisions in their capacities as corporate fiduciaries, must act in the same manner as a reasonably prudent person in their position would.

The <u>duty of loyalty</u> stands for the principle that directors and officers of a corporation in making all decisions in their capacities as corporate fiduciaries, must act without personal economic conflict.

The <u>duty of loyalty</u> can be breached either by making a self-interested transaction or the taking of a corporate opportunity.

The *business judgment rule* stands for the principle that courts will not second guess the business judgment of corporate managers and will find the duty of care has been met so long as the fiduciary executed a reasonably informed, good faith, rational judgment without the presence of a conflict of interest.

Your compliance with these basic legal principles is the foundation that guides and protects all of your activities and decisions as a board member.

Finally, you should also be aware that numerous lawsuits over the years have tested whether a given board or its members have properly observed these duties of care and of loyalty. That is why you must always insist on the protection of a strong indemnification provision in your bank's bylaws and directors' and officers' liability insurance in a sufficient amount to cover anticipated exposures.

#   #   #

Chapter One

Invited to Join a Bank Board?
Should You Accept?

*"We make a living by what we get,
we make a life by what we give."*

Sir Winston Churchill

In many respects, the banking industry has become the favorite 'piñata' of politicians, the media and the public; everyone feels entitled to take a swipe. The 2007-09 financial crisis seriously damaged the image of the entire banking industry including the reputations of both bankers and bank directors.

Today over 5,000 regional and community banks serve their customers and communities throughout our nation. These banks not only survived the crisis but the vast majority remained profitable and they continue to serve the financial needs of their customers.

All financial institutions may have been painted with the same "Wall Street" brush by the media but most regional and community banks remained on solid footing and continue to support economic growth.

Serving as a bank director may have been considered an honor in the past - but times have changed. Accepting such a position today requires careful consideration. This book explores some of the many pros and cons of serving on a bank board and provides a roadmap for making your job more rewarding.

Despite the risks, I still encourage you to serve on a bank board that meets your personal due diligence requirements and that will benefit from your personal experience and skill set.

The most significant challenge faced by banking today is attracting talented people to such an unpopular industry. Bank directors serve an important and unique role and it's especially important that community banks attract and retain talented people on their boards. Hopefully, this book will help you decide if you are one of these people.

The banking system provides the financial liquidity required to support our nation's economic activity and job growth. Some politicians don't seem to understand that our nation's banks provide the oil for our nation's economic engine and without oil an engine won't run.

Community banks have a special relationship with "small business" and economic reports indicate that the majority of job growth is provided by small business. Community banks are best positioned to serve the financial needs of small business and support future job growth.

From a personal perspective this chapter addresses the key factors I consider before accepting or declining an invitation to serve on a bank board. My experience [page 105] includes serving as a financial executive at two regional banking institutions, board service at four banks and directorships at two non-financial companies.

The job of a bank director continues to evolve and become more complex with an ever-increasing number of banking rules and regulations to consider. Doing your personal due-diligence and gaining an understanding of the scope of regulatory requirements helps avoid surprises as you engage in bank board activities.

Oversight of regulatory compliance may be an essential part of a bank director's job but it can also be a significant distraction to your oversight of corporate strategy and financial performance. Be prepared for a substantial time commitment, as bank boards tend to meet more frequently than non-financial boards as result of this higher level of regulatory oversight. Serving on board committees will also add to your time commitments to your bank.

Don't expect your increased time commitment to be offset by your board compensation. National studies continue to report that regional and community bank directors tend to be compensated at lower levels than board members of non-financial corporations of similar size.

Also, expect your personal attorney to tell you that your increased time commitment will be accompanied by more personal liability than board members of non-financial corporations due to a bank director's higher regulatory exposure. As a result, you will want to make certain the bank has a robust directors' & officers' [D&O] insurance policy and strong by-law indemnification to protect you as much as possible.

You will also see media reports describing how the Federal Deposit Insurance Corporation [FDIC] takes legal action to recover losses from bank officers and directors at failed banks. The study [page 109] published by the American Association of Bank Directors [AABD] found such claims are generally made against board members because they approved loans that ultimately went bad. Therefore, the AABD suggests board members do not approve individual loans, except as required by law. [Chapter Fourteen]

As described in Chapter Two, the most important element of your due-diligence process is gaining confidence in the leadership and integrity of the bank's board members and management team. We all know that people are the key element that will make or break any business. Take the time to personally evaluate the other board members and gain an understanding of the management team's strategy and abilities and the bank's performance.

Your decision to become a bank director also requires some self-evaluation. As described in Chapter Six, a successful bank requires a quality mix of people and talent. Do you add value to the board or do you duplicate existing skills?

In my experience the most effective boards tended to be relatively small with 8 to 12 members; therefore, every seat is important. Consider that you might not be the right person to occupy a board seat even though the other board members may want you to join or remain on a board. A board functions best when it is not composed solely of people who all "think alike". Your self-evaluation needs to be an ongoing process and you should recognize when it's time for you to depart.

Accept a board seat [or remain on a board] only when you are comfortable with your duties as a bank director; the time commitment, the board structure and, most important, that you have complete confidence in the integrity of other board members and the management team. Over time you are building personal and professional relationships with all of these individuals and they are the key to your bank's future success.

As a bank director you have a window to view economic activity in your regional and local markets. No other business interacts with every other type of business in the communities served by your bank. Your bank's customer and credit strategy will have a direct impact on the lives and jobs of people throughout your markets.

Rapidly changing technology is changing financial competition and the way banks and non-banks deliver financial services and how customers utilize these services. Competition is no longer just local and large national organizations can reach into any market with acquisitions and technology. You will find understanding this new competitive environment is more challenging than the evolving regulatory environment.

As described in Chapter Sixteen, many banks faced with increasing competition and higher costs due to increased regulatory requirements will elect to be acquired. Other bankers will see an opportunity to be an acquiror and grow. Bank directors will constantly be faced with this very challenging strategic decision that impacts shareholders, customers, employees and their communities.

Banking is a very dynamic business and successful banks require boards and management teams with a wide range of experience, knowledge and skills to successfully address changing conditions.

Your service as a bank director provides you with a unique opportunity to contribute your insight and personal skills to an institution that is an essential ingredient to the economic health of your community.

If you are up to the task then your job as a bank director will be very rewarding.

# # #

"Choose Wisely."

Movie: Indiana Jones

Chapter Two

Management & Tone at the Top

*"Quality means doing it right
when no one is looking."*

Henry Ford

Management and "Tone at the Top" starts with your bank's Chief Executive Officer [CEO]. If your bank's CEO doesn't have an ethical mindset you should not join the board and if you are a current board member then you need to take steps to replace your CEO or resign. You must trust that your CEO is always dedicated to "doing the right thing".

Your CEO sets the "tone" for the rest of your management team and that "tone" is transmitted to every employee. Unfortunately, we all recognize that from time-to-time an employee will not do the "right thing". Having the right tone sets the stage for management at any level to correct or replace such an employee.

Any failure to act can have significant repercussions on your bank, your management, your board and your personal reputation. The negative financial and reputational impact of a failure to act is clearly illustrated by the well-documented case of management pressure on employees that resulted in the unauthorized account opening scandal at Wells Fargo Bank.

Your board's role in setting the right "tone" cannot be overstated and all board members must also be committed to "doing the right thing".

The negative public perception of all financial institutions is a significant problem today. According to a 2016 Gallup Survey, less than 30 percent of bank customers have a "great deal" of confidence in banking institutions.

Today's reality is that bankers are not popular and banks have not regained the trust of bank customers.

As a bank director, it is mandatory that your management team is focused on doing the right thing for your customers. Take the opportunity to look at your bank's products and services from the viewpoint of your customers – not just your accounting staff. For example:

> *Do your services and fees really appear to be understandable and fair?*

> *Would you bank with your institution if you were not a director? If not - why not?*

Management Styles

This chapter does not attempt to explain how to be a great leader. Churchill was considered a great leader during World War II but was voted out of office in peacetime.

Circumstances dictate leadership requirements and history shows that effective leaders have had many styles, personalities, backgrounds, etc.

Churchill clearly communicated a common objective that every UK citizen understood during the war. It is important for a leader to be able to communicate a clear sense of mission or objective.

Two other essential components of leadership in my view are mutual trust and respect. These attributes are earned, not learned.

Personally, I don't believe that the "command and control" method of leadership works. At Sunbeam Corporation, Al Dunlap was "in charge" and management through fear, not respect, was the dominant force. The results were catastrophic and ultimately led to corporate bankruptcy.

The following example of an effective CEO was published in my earlier book, "It Is What It Is", the story about saving AmericanWest Bank during the 2007-09 financial crisis.

What separated AmericanWest Bank from the more than 300 other banks that failed during the financial crisis?

Leadership at every level made a difference. So a few observations on the bank's leadership in general and Pat Rusnak's [President & CEO] leadership style seem appropriate.

The "Tone at the Top" was visible and consistent. Rusnak's approach to dealing with problems was contagious; accept the facts ["It Is What It Is"], don't wallow in denial, don't waste time with the "blame game", identify and implement a solution.

Decisions were made - not deferred or avoided. Once the facts were clear Rusnak's decisions were implemented and supported. Management changes, closing branch offices, staff reductions, problem loan recognition, foreclosed property sales and other tough decisions were made promptly and communicated. This was true at all levels - the board, executive management and operating management.

Bank employees got the message – authority for operating decisions was delegated down to the appropriate level - not delegated up to the CEO or the board.

Rusnak led by example – he was visible to other employees throughout the bank and no doubt word traveled that he worked as hard and as long as anybody in the organization. Frequent all-employee conference calls with Rusnak that included open questions and candid answers kept employees informed and engaged.

The board and Rusnak always kept an "open mind" and sought the best advice available. Rusnak didn't try to impress others with how much he knew; he asked questions and wanted to learn what others knew about a topic. He constantly spoke with a wide variety of people [bankers, attorneys, accountants, investment bankers, consultants and bank regulators] and consistently asked questions to learn more about the topic at hand.

The bank avoided corporate "perks" in an age of sacrifice. The bank had no company aircraft and Rusnak drove his own pickup truck, not a company owned luxury car. He didn't even have a reserved parking space.

The negative reaction witnessed at other banks when tone-deaf corporate executives arrive in the company airplane or a company owned luxury automobile to announce expense cuts and employee layoffs did not occur at AmericanWest.

Qualified bankers were in short supply and throughout this troubled period Rusnak and his management team were not only able to retain talented employees but also attract talented people. Even in the toughest of times Rusnak kept a "can do" constructive attitude and the bank survived.

# # #

"Attitude is a little thing that makes a big difference."

Winston Churchill

Chapter Three

Your Bank's Management Team

*"Success in management requires
learning as fast as the world is changing."*

Warren Bennis

Your bank's strategic plan and annual operating plan [budget] are meaningless if you don't have an executive management team that understands your objectives and is committed to working together to achieve those objectives.

In my experience effective leaders hire quality people and trust these people to do a quality job – effective leaders don't "micro-manage" staff. As a bank executive I always expected my staff to know more about their jobs than I did and if I had to tell a staff member how to do their job then I had hired the wrong employee.

Mutual trust and respect between executive management and your board certainly helps produce a team that works together. Mutual respect is a two-way street and includes respect for each person's talent, experience, opinions, gender, etc.

Your bank's executive management team will consist of a number of key positions that may or may not be described by one of the following functional titles. Officer titles don't always indicate an employee's function as most banks utilize a wide variety of officer titles: president, executive vice president, senior vice president, vice president, assistant vice president, associate vice president, cashier, assistant cashier, treasurer, etc.

The following descriptive titles represent some of your bank's important management functions with related descriptions of that officer's typical duties that help provide effective management of your bank's operations.

Chief Executive Officer

The CEO is the highest-ranking executive in your bank with the primary responsibility for making day-to-day decisions, managing the overall operations and resources of the bank, and acting as the main point of communication between your board [Lead Director – Chapter Five] and the other members of management.

Chief Financial Officer

A CFO is the senior executive responsible for managing the financial activities of your bank. Typical CFO duties include management of accounting, budgeting, asset/liability, liquidity and the investment portfolio.

Your CFO may also lead the strategic planning process and, in some institutions, be responsible for bank operations.

Chief Credit Officer

A CCO is responsible for managing your bank's credit policy, credit analysis, credit approval process and problem credits. Your CCO should not make loans; your CCO's job is to provide an independent "check and balance" for your bank's credit exposure.

Your bank's loan officers are responsible for originating new loans, renewing customer loans and submitting those loans to the CCO [staff] for credit analysis. Your CCO is then responsible for making independent recommendations to a management loan approval committee for approval or rejection of each loan.

To be effective, your CCO must have authority to reject any loan with inadequate credit characteristics. The CCO needs to be objective, and his/her compensation should only be tied to credit quality and not to loan growth. Confidence in your bank's CCO and your understanding of your bank's credit and loan approval process is absolutely necessary.

Chief Lending Officer

Your CLO is typically the executive responsible for bank-wide loan origination and the renewal of loans for all commercial and consumer customers.

If you are a director of a larger institution then your bank may assign responsibility for specific customer segments and loan categories to separate executive officers.

Whatever your organizational structure, any executive officer responsible for the origination and renewal of loans is a critical member of your bank's management team.

Chief Operations Officer

Your COO, if your bank has this position, may be responsible for any number of bank operations, such as: information technology & security, loan operations, deposit operations and/or branch operations.

This executive is charged with the management of efficient bank-wide operations that meet all regulatory compliance requirements.

In smaller banks these functions may be assigned to the CFO and/or other executive with operating responsibilities.

Senior Compliance Officer

Your SCO is typically responsible for the management of regulatory compliance within your bank. In this regard, the SCO is generally working in an operating capacity and, as a result, the SCO cannot be expected to also perform the compliance audit function.

Internal Audit Officer

Your bank's internal auditor independently evaluates management's compliance with risk management policy, internal controls [including compliance with laws and regulations] and operating procedures and processes.

Internal audit must be independent from all activities evaluated and have direct reporting access to your board's audit committee.

#   #   #

As a bank director you should clearly understand your bank's executive management organization, executive responsibilities and you must have confidence in the professional skills and integrity of your bank's executive management team.

Chapter Four

Your Job as a Bank Director

*"I try not to miss the big ideas,
forget the little ones, and try to get them right.
End of job description."*

Jeremy Grantham

As a bank director you have a variety of constituents to consider: your shareholders [they elect you], regulators, management, employees, customers and your community. Managing your relationships with each of these groups requires you to exercise your "duty of care" [page 13] to avoid exposing yourself to unnecessary liability.

Your bank's corporate structure provides a clear distinction between the role of management and your role as a board member. Your CEO is responsible for the day-to-day operation of the bank subject to oversight by your board of directors.

Your board conducts discussions and makes decisions as a group and all of your confidential board discussions and decisions are to be made in the privacy of your boardroom.

The other chapters in this book more fully describe your responsibilities as a board member. The following points describe what **_you are not to do_** as a board member.

Direct input by you, as an individual board member, into management's day-to-day decisions and/or operations circumvents the responsibilities of your fellow board members. Such individual action on your part is inappropriate and disrespectful to each of your fellow board members and can expose you to liability.

In that regard, it is important that each board member respect management's role and not attempt to "step into the shoes" of management. Such inappropriate actions are not only disrespectful and disruptive to your board, management and bank operations but may also create unnecessary liability for the individual bank director.

As a board member it is appropriate for you to listen if/when a shareholder, customer or employee approaches you concerning a bank related issue. However, it is not appropriate for you to express an opinion and appear to make a decision on behalf of your bank.

As a bank director you must be very careful to avoid becoming personally involved in bank customer or bank personnel matters – it's not your job as a board member. This is especially awkward if you also have a personal relationship with a bank customer or employee.

If you express your opinion as a bank director then you risk creating an unnecessary obligation of behalf of your bank concerning the customer, employee or shareholder's personal agenda.

You need to avoid getting personally "trapped" or "trapping" your board; there is always more to their story!

You should promptly bring any significant customer, employee or shareholder issue to the attention of your CEO, Lead Director or, if appropriate, your board.

#   #   #

Chapter Five

Board Leadership

"A sense of humor is part of the art of leadership, of getting along with people, of getting things done."

Dwight D. Eisenhower
President 1953 -1961

Board Leadership

The 2007-09 financial crisis turned the spotlight on independent board leadership. Every board is [or should be] comprised of individuals with different personalities, experience levels and professional backgrounds; there is no "right answer" for every board. This chapter provides a few thoughts and suggestions for you and your board to consider.

First, don't confuse "control" with "leadership skills". The concept of a "split" role between the CEO and a board Chairman or Lead Director is now considered "best practice". However, defining this relationship is critical to effective board governance.

It's important to recognize the difference between individuals [in either role] that want to control the flow of board information and decision making with those individuals that exhibit the open leadership skills required for effective board engagement and oversight.

It's a serious "red flag" if your CEO ignores board policy or your independent Chairman or Lead Director is engaging in day-to-day management decisions.

Any attempt by any board member to control or suppress information and play politics to subvert management authority (hiring, termination, new loan, etc.) in "private" must promptly be disclosed to the full board.

Any attempt by any executive or board member to subvert the balance of authority between management and your board calls for an executive session of your board to address the issue.

Lead Director or Chairman?

It's now considered "best practice" to have an independent director [non-management] as the board's leader. Function is far more important than title and I have witnessed Lead Directors, Presiding Directors and non-management Chairmen provide effective board leadership.

Effective boards are always a work in progress and title is not as important as the skillful board leadership required to help your board adapt to changing circumstances.

Many banks have already combined the Chairman/CEO title so this book will refer to a "Lead Director" to describe the independent non-management individual elected to provide board leadership. What is generally not accepted in today's climate is a combination Chairman/CEO without a separate Lead Director. Absence of any independent board leadership should be a "red flag" and a reason not to join a particular bank board.

Your Lead Director's Job

Your Lead Director has the potential to improve the effectiveness of your board or to degrade it. It's essential that an atmosphere of mutual respect exists between your Lead Director, every member of your board and your bank's executive management team - especially between your Lead Director and your CEO.

The duties of your Lead Director would typically include the following responsibilities:

> Chair all of your board meetings and executive sessions. The Lead Director must chair executive sessions in which

the CEO is not present. If the CEO resists this practice, this should be a "red flag".

> Coordinate agendas with your CEO to ensure that all appropriate information is provided for timely consideration by your board.

> Encourage communication and facilitate questions during your board meetings.

> Lead your executive sessions and encourage every board member to provide feedback.

> Provide feedback from executive sessions to your CEO.

Your Lead Director is not a member of your bank's management team and your Lead Director must avoid stepping into the shoes of management.

The essential role of independent oversight is lost if your Lead Director becomes involved in day-to-day management decisions. Your Lead Director, like every other board member, has just one vote.

#   #   #

Chapter Six

Board Member Selection

"Choose Wisely."

Movie: Indiana Jones

The most important job of your board is having the courage to recruit and retain a balanced mix of qualified people as directors. When you have the right people on your board then your board will also select an excellent CEO and have the courage to act if it's necessary to replace your CEO or a board member.

The nominating & governance committee [Nom/Gov] is typically charged with the identification and recruitment of new board members. However, every bank director needs to fully appreciate the importance of consistently having the right mix of talented people on your board.

Board Size & Membership

Experience indicates smaller boards with 8 to 12 members are more effective than larger boards. In addition, I suggest your CEO be the only management member of your board. This size and membership structure also provides sufficient independent board members to serve on board committees.

The skill sets of individual bank board members needed to provide effective bank oversight continue to evolve. Your starting point for recruiting and retaining an effective board is a simple skill set matrix used to identify the professional skills required of your bank's individual board members.

The following example lists the required board skills down the left and board members [initials] across the top. Your goal is to identify what skills your board needs – not justify the skills you already have on your current board.

You should start today if your bank has not utilized this simple tool to identify the professional skills required of your bank's individual board members.

Board Skill	ABC	DEF	GHI	JKL	MNO	PQR
Finance			X			
Technology						
Marketing						
Legal	X			X		
Real Estate		X			X	

The days are long past when the primary function of bank board members was developing new business and approving loans. It's not whom you know but what you know that counts today.

Your bank's Nom/Gov committee [Chapter Twelve] typically has the responsibility for soliciting input from all board members and from your management team to identify the skills necessary for an effective board.

Once Nom/Gov has identified the skills required, it's time for the committee to identify the skills you have and don't have on your board today. It's important to identify and avoid duplication – for example, as in the preceding example; do you have multiple attorneys or real estate developers? Do you have a "nice" or "legacy" person [PQR] on your board without any of the required skills?

In recruiting board members to serve on the Audit Committee [Chapter Ten], it is important to select persons who qualify as "financially literate"; that is, they must be able to read and understand financial statements, audit reports, etc. While that may be a good qualification for all board members, it is essential for Audit Committee members. At least one person needs to be selected who can chair the Audit Committee, and that person should qualify as a "financial expert".

Sarbanes Oxley rules for publicly traded companies describe a financial expert as: "a person who has the following attributes: [i] an understanding of generally accepted accounting principles and financial statements; [ii] the ability to assess the general application of such principles in connection with the accounting for estimates, accruals and reserves; [iii] experience preparing, auditing, analyzing or evaluating financial statements that present a breadth and level of complexity of accounting issues that are generally comparable to the breadth and complexity of issues that can reasonably be expected to be raised by the [bank's] financial statements, or experience actively supervising one or more persons engaged in such activities; [iv] an understanding of internal controls and procedures for financial reporting; and [v] an understanding of audit committee functions."

A good example of such a person would typically be a CPA, financial executive or corporate attorney, as long as that person has the attributes described above.

Another hot topic today is board diversity including gender, age and length of service. For example, would your board benefit with the addition of a younger female with technology or marketing experience?

Smaller boards with the required skill sets tend to be the most effective boards. As a result, duplication and lack of required skills wastes important board seats. Don't utilize a skill set matrix if you don't have the courage to act.

Board Assessments

If your Nom/Gov committee has not already initiated an annual board assessment then it is time to start.

Board assessments are a sensitive topic and candor is frequently in short supply – especially when it comes to peer review and self-evaluation. Board assessments without individual candor are a waste of time. Providing your honest opinion of other board members' skills and performing a candid self-evaluation are the foundation for an effective board assessment.

Replacing a board member is certainly not fun. It's very tough to ask a colleague to resign or not stand for re-election. You expect management to replace a poor performer – but, it's easier to tell management that they need to act than to do it yourself. However, boards have the same responsibility as management.

In addition, this is the time for you to ask yourself if you really provide an essential skill for your bank's board or is it time for you to depart?

Frequently an independent third-party assessment can be helpful – sometimes not. Board members generally recognize the changes that should be made but are just reluctant to act. A third-party can provide your board with confidential feedback and a reason to act, but don't request a candid appraisal if you are not prepared to act.

#   #   #

"Be Careful What You Wish For."

Chinese Proverb

Chapter Seven

Your Board Meetings

"If you had to identify, in one word, the reason why the human race has not achieved, and never will achieve, its full potential, that word would be 'meetings'."

Dave Barry

Your Lead Director is your board's designated contact with your bank's CEO. As described in Chapter Five, your Lead Director should chair all your board meetings, work with your CEO to make certain board agendas address every important topic and provide feedback from all board members to the CEO.

The following steps provide the framework for your Lead Director's leadership of your board meetings:

Your Meeting Agendas

Your board meetings provide an excellent forum for directors to assess the depth of the executive management team. As a result, your bank's executive officers should attend and provide regular reports at every board meeting.

Step 1: Lead Director conducts formal board meeting with the executive management team in attendance. Your CEO coordinates the reports and presentations made by your bank's executives. All of the bank's board members have an opportunity to question executives during this meeting.

Board minutes will document the presentations, general discussions and any action taken during this board session.

Step 2: The Lead Director should excuse all non-board members as a group when all management reports are completed. This is your opportunity as bank directors to discuss any bank related issue with your CEO in private.

Minutes are not required during this session unless the board takes specific action that requires documentation by your Lead Director or CEO.

Step 3: Your board conducts a "executive session" without your CEO – the CEO is now excused. Your Lead Director goes around your board table asking each board member if they have anything they wish to discuss.

This is the opportunity for every board member to raise any issue or concern. Your executive session is conducted to avoid unnecessary "parking lot" conversations between individual board members after the meeting.

All of your board members have a responsibility to allow adequate time for the executive session and not "rush out" at the end of board meetings to attend other matters.

Minutes are not required during your executive session unless the board takes specific action that requires documentation by your Lead Director.

Step 4: Your Lead Director discusses the executive session and any board concerns with the CEO as soon as possible after the conclusion of the board meeting.

Your Executive Sessions

Some CEOs and board members don't think a "regular" executive session is really necessary. However, experience indicates that regular executive sessions at the end of every board meeting are in everyone's best interest. It is a good discipline to establish that such a session will be held at the end of every board meeting, even if the session turns out to be short and nothing of substance is discussed at a given meeting.

CEOs and board members must recognize that directors will discuss bank business with one another informally [at social events, their clubs, etc.] if a regular time and location for private discussion is not provided. Regular executive sessions help prevent "lobbying" by individual directors outside the boardroom.

Your executive session is the proper time and place for the Lead Director to ask each director if they have anything they wish to discuss. It is important for your board members to limit discussion to important policy topics.

The executive session is not a forum for petty issues or personal grievances. The executive session is not an excuse for your board to become involved in day-to-day management issues. It is essential that your board members avoid unintended conflict and respect the roles of the CEO and bank management.

It's also important for your board members to remember the boardroom is a "fish bowl", everyone knows you are in executive session. For this reason, a regular executive session at the end of every board meeting becomes "routine", not "special".

Your board members need to be sensitive to the potential "unintended consequences" of a long executive session. You should open the door when business is done, this is not the time or place for directors to have a prolonged discussion about a sporting event.

Your Lead Director must always brief the CEO immediately after the executive session on the topics discussed during your meeting. This follow-up is essential to maintaining positive CEO-board relations and needs to occur even if no topic of substance was discussed.

#   #   #

Chapter Eight

Bank Regulatory Exams & Orders

*"Life is like a box of chocolates;
you never know what you're gonna get."*

Movie: Forrest Gump

Bank regulators conduct periodic examinations of all financial institutions. The primary focus of regulatory examinations is the safety and soundness of the financial system, including your bank. Bank regulators also examine your bank's compliance with all applicable banking laws, banking regulations and bank regulatory rules.

Your bank's compliance with bank regulations is a given – you have no choice. As discussed in Chapter Thirteen, many bank regulations state "management and the board shall" comply with little or no distinction between the roles of your management and your board.

Your bank is subject to regulatory oversight by the FDIC as described in the following section. Your bank is most likely a subsidiary of a bank holding company, which is subject to regulatory oversight by the Federal Reserve System. As a practical matter, your duties and responsibilities as a board member of your holding company and bank are identical.

The FDIC regulatory examination process for your bank covers a wide-range of activities and bank regulators have made it clear that bank directors are ultimately responsible if management fails to comply with bank regulations.

The remainder of this chapter contains excerpts from the 2017 Edition of the **Manual of Examination Policies** *published by the Federal Deposit Insurance Corporation [FDIC]. These excerpts only summarize a few key elements of the FDIC examination and enforcement process. Complete and updated policies are available at FDIC.gov*

Bank Regulatory Examinations

The Federal Deposit Insurance Corporation conducts bank examinations to ensure public confidence in the banking system and to protect the Deposit Insurance Fund.

Maintaining public confidence in the banking system is essential because customer deposits are a primary funding source that depository institutions use to meet fundamental objectives such as providing financial services.

Safeguarding the integrity of the Deposit Insurance Fund is necessary to protect customers' deposits and to resolve failed banks. On-site examinations help ensure the stability of insured depository institutions by identifying undue risks and weak risk management practices.

Examination activities center on evaluating an institution's **C**apital, **A**sset quality, **M**anagement, **E**arnings, **L**iquidity, and **S**ensitivity to market risk. [*Your bank's CAMELS Rating*]

Evaluating a bank's adherence to laws and regulations is also an important part of bank examinations and is given high priority by Congress and bank supervisors.

Bank examinations play a key role in the supervisory process by helping the FDIC identify emerging risks in the financial-services industry.

Full-Scope [*Safety & Soundness*] Exam

Bank examiners focus their resources on a bank's highest risk areas when assessing risk management programs, financial conditions, internal controls, etc. The exercise of examiner judgment to determine the scope and depth of review in each functional area is crucial to the success of the risk-focused supervisory process.

A full-scope examination represents the bank regulator's evaluation of Bank Capital, Asset Quality, Management, Earnings, Liquidity, and Sensitivity to Market Risk. [*CAMELS*].

Composite and component [*CAMELS*] ratings are assigned based on a numerical scale from 1 to 5, with 1 indicating the highest rating, strongest performance and risk management practices, and least degree of supervisory concern. A 5 rating indicates the lowest rating, weakest performance and risk management practices, and highest degree of supervisory concern.

In a full-scope examination, all examination activities are considered in the overall assessment of the institution. These activities include the Risk Management, IT, Bank Secrecy Act [BSA]/Anti-Money Laundering [AML]/ Office of Foreign Assets Control, Trust, Registered Transfer Agent, Municipal Securities Dealer, and Government Securities Dealer examination programs.

Compliance and Community Reinvestment Act examination activities are included in the overall supervision program with separate reports and examination cycles.

Examination ratings [*CAMELS*] and summary comments are included in the Report of Examination [ROE].

CAMELS Ratings
Capital Adequacy

A financial institution is expected to maintain capital commensurate with the nature and extent of risks to the institution and the ability of management to identify, measure, monitor, and control these risks.

The effects of credit, market, and other risks on the institution's financial condition are considered when bank regulators evaluate the adequacy of capital.

The types and quantity of risk inherent in an institution's activities will determine the extent to which it may be necessary to maintain capital at levels above required regulatory minimums to properly reflect the potentially adverse consequences that these risks may have on the institution's capital.

Asset Quality

The asset quality rating reflects the quantity of existing and potential credit risk associated with the loan and investment portfolios, other real estate owned, and other assets, as well as off-balance sheet transactions.

The ability of management to identify, measure, monitor, and control credit risk is also reflected here. The evaluation of asset quality should consider the adequacy of the allowance for loan and lease losses and weigh the exposure to counter-party, issuer, or borrower default under actual or implied contractual agreements.

All other risks that may affect the value or marketability of an institution's assets, including, but not limited to, operating, market, reputation, strategic, or compliance risks, should also be considered.

Management

The capability of the board of directors and management, in their respective roles, to identify, measure, monitor, and control the risks of an institution's activities and to ensure a financial institution's safe, sound, and efficient operation in compliance with applicable laws and regulations is reflected in this rating.

Senior management is responsible for developing and implementing policies, procedures, and practices that translate the board's goals, objectives, and risk limits into prudent operating standards.

Generally, directors need not be actively involved in day-to-day operations; however, they must provide clear guidance regarding acceptable risk exposure levels and ensure that appropriate policies, procedures, and practices have been established.

> *It's important for bank directors to recognize that the regulatory evaluation of your board is included in the management rating – it's not just a management rating.*

Earnings

This rating reflects not only the quantity and trend of earnings, but also factors that may affect the sustainability or quality of earnings.

The quantity as well as the quality of earnings can be affected by excessive or inadequately managed credit risk that may result in loan losses and require additions to the Allowance of Loan and Lease Losses [ALLL], or by high levels of market risk that may unduly expose an institution's earnings to volatility in interest rates.

The quality of earnings may also be diminished by undue reliance on extraordinary gains, nonrecurring events, or favorable tax effects. Future earnings may be adversely affected by an inability to forecast or control funding and operating expenses, improperly executed or ill-advised business strategies, or poorly managed or uncontrolled exposure to other risks.

Liquidity

In evaluating the adequacy of a financial institution's liquidity position, consideration is given to the current level and prospective sources of liquidity compared to funding needs, as well as to the adequacy of funds management practices relative to the institution's size, complexity, and risk profile.

In general, funds management practices should ensure that an institution is able to maintain a level of liquidity sufficient to meet its financial obligations in a timely manner and to fulfill the legitimate banking needs of its community.

Funds management practices should reflect the ability of the institution to manage unplanned changes in funding sources, as well as react to changes in market conditions that affect the ability to quickly liquidate assets with minimal loss.

In addition, funds management practices should ensure that liquidity is not maintained at a high cost, or through undue reliance on funding sources that may not be available in times of financial stress or adverse changes in market conditions.

Sensitivity to Market Risk

The sensitivity to market risk component reflects the degree to which changes in interest rates, foreign exchange rates, commodity prices, or equity prices can adversely affect a financial institution's earnings or economic capital.

When evaluating this component, consideration should be given to management's ability to identify, measure, monitor, and control market risk; the institution's size; the nature and complexity of its activities; and the adequacy of its capital and earnings in relation to its level of market risk exposure.

Other Regulatory Examinations

Information Technology Examination

Information technology [IT] services apply to virtually all recordkeeping and operational areas in banks. These IT services may be managed internally on a bank's own in-house computer system, or outsourced, wholly or in part, to an independent data center that performs most IT functions. Although some or all IT services may be outsourced, management and the board retain oversight responsibilities.

The potential consequences of receiving faulty data or suffering an interruption of services are serious and warrant comprehensive IT policies and procedures and thorough IT examinations.

A primary objective of an IT examination is to determine the confidentiality, integrity, and availability of records produced by automated systems. Examination priorities include an evaluation of management's ability to identify risks and maintain appropriate compensating controls.

Bank Secrecy Act Examination

The Financial Recordkeeping and Reporting of Currency and Foreign Transactions Act of 1970 is often referred to as the Bank

Secrecy Act [BSA]. The purpose of the BSA is to ensure U.S. financial institutions maintain appropriate records and file certain reports involving currency transactions and customer relationships.

Several acts and regulations that strengthen the scope and enforcement of BSA, anti-money laundering [AML], and counter-terrorist-financing measures have been signed into law.

Consumer Protection Examination

The principal objective of consumer protection examinations is to determine a bank's compliance with various consumer and civil rights laws and regulations.

Consumer protection statutes include, but are not limited to, Truth in Lending, Truth in Savings, Community Reinvestment Act, and Fair Housing regulations.

Noncompliance with these regulatory restrictions and standards may result in an injustice to affected individual(s) and reflects adversely on an institution's management and reputation.

Moreover, violations of consumer laws can result in civil or criminal liabilities, and consequently, financial penalties.

Trust Department Examination [If Applicable]

A bank's trust department acts in a fiduciary capacity when the assets it manages are not the bank's, but belong to and are for the benefit of others. This type of relationship necessitates a great deal of confidence on the part of customers and demands a high degree of good faith.

Reports of Examination [ROE]

The Reports of Examination [ROE] are highly confidential.

Although a copy is provided to a bank, that copy remains the property of the FDIC. Without the FDIC's prior authorization, directors, officers, employees, and agents of a bank are not permitted to disclose the contents of a report. Under specified circumstances,

FDIC regulations permit disclosures by a bank to its parent holding company or majority shareholder.

Standard FDIC regulations do not prohibit employees or agents of a bank from reviewing the ROE if it is necessary for purposes of their employment. Accountants and attorneys acting in their capacities as bank employees or agents may review an examination report without prior FDIC approval, but only insofar as it relates to their scope of employment.

Discussions with Management & Directors

Generally, the examiner-in-charge [EIC] will discuss the recommended component and composite ratings with senior management and, when appropriate, the board of directors, near the conclusion of the examination. Examiners should clearly explain that their ratings are tentative and subject to the review and final approval by the regional director.

Examiners follow regional guidance regarding the disclosure of component and composite ratings of 3 or worse. Generally, in these situations, examiners will contact the regional office overseeing the institution and discuss the proposed ratings with the case manager or assistant regional director prior to disclosing the ratings to management or the board.

Management Meeting

All major examination issues should be discussed with senior management as soon as practical during an examination. At a minimum, all significant issues should be discussed at the end of the examination, prior to meeting with the board of directors.

Meetings with Directors

Your bank's CEO should encourage you as a director to attend meetings with bank regulators - such meetings will help you better understand any regulatory concerns and appreciate your CEO's responses to bank regulators.

FDIC policies have been established for meetings with boards of directors. These policies are designed to encourage director involvement in, and enhance director awareness of, FDIC supervisory efforts and to increase the effectiveness of such efforts.

The bank's composite rating is the most important variable in deciding if and when these meetings should be held.

> *Don't be defensive. It's important for your management and board members to recognize that bank examiners are evaluating institutions throughout their jurisdiction and are seeing emerging risks that may not be evident to you.*

FDIC Enforcement Actions

Regulatory agencies may use formal or informal procedures to address weak operating practices, deteriorating financial conditions, or apparent violations of laws or regulations.

A financial institution's failure to implement the corrective measures detailed in an informal agreement may lead to formal corrective actions.

Memorandum of Understanding [MOU]

A memorandum of understanding [MOU] is a common informal agreement used by the FDIC to obtain a commitment from a bank's board of directors to implement corrective measures.

Other informal actions include board resolutions, letter agreements, and other forms of bilateral agreements or unilateral actions. Informal actions are not public information or legally enforceable.

An MOU provides a structured way to correct problems at institutions that have moderate weaknesses, but have not deteriorated to a point requiring formal corrective actions.

An MOU may be used to address specific problems at institutions rated 1 or 2 and should, at a minimum, be considered for all institutions rated 3.

The FDIC may request management to submit a Compliance Plan. The plan must describe the steps the institution will take to correct identified deficiencies and the time frames for completing the steps.

If an institution fails to submit a requested plan or fails to adhere to a submitted plan, the FDIC will pursue formal enforcement action.

Consent Order

The FDIC is authorized to take certain formal enforcement actions when unsafe or unsound practices or conditions exist. The concept of unsafe or unsound practices or conditions touches upon a bank's entire operations, and a single definition would not capture the broad spectrum of activities or conditions included in the term.

If an institution agrees to comply with an enforcement action [stipulates], the FDIC will issue a consent order. However, if an institution does not stipulate, the FDIC may pursue a cease and desist order. Both actions generally contain the same corrective provisions and are public documents.

By stipulating, the institution waives its right to an administrative hearing. Eliminating the administrative hearing allows the institution to avoid lengthy and costly legal proceedings and allows the FDIC to address unsafe or unsound practices and violations more quickly.

By stipulating to the action, the institution consents to the enforcement action without admitting or denying engagement in unsafe or unsound practices or violations.

Cease and Desist Order

The purpose of a cease and desist order is to remedy unsafe or unsound practices or violations and to correct conditions resulting from such practices or violations. Formal actions may be pursued before a violation or unsafe or unsound practice occurs in order to prevent a developing situation from reaching more serious proportions.

Examiners are required to review a bank's compliance with any outstanding order during examinations. Orders typically require a bank to submit certain documents, including progress reports, to the regional office.

Civil Money Penalties

The Financial Institutions Reform, Recovery, and Enforcement Act of 1989 [FIRREA] significantly increased the penalties for both banks and individuals and broadened the applicability of civil money penalties.

Civil money penalties may be assessed for the violation of any law or regulation, any final order or temporary order issued, any condition imposed in writing by the appropriate Federal banking agency in connection with the approval of any application, and any written agreement between a depository institution and Federal banking agency.

Civil money penalties are assessed not only to punish the violator according to the degree of culpability and severity of the violation, but also to deter future violations.

It is the FDIC's policy that, whenever a violation committed by an individual results in personal financial or economic gain and/or financial loss to the bank, the amount involved shall be repaid as a portion of the penalty assessment or, preferably, through restitution to the bank if the bank suffered a loss.

Federal Reserve System

As stated earlier in this chapter, your bank is most likely a subsidiary of a bank holding company, which is subject to regulatory oversight by the Federal Reserve System. As a practical matter, your responsibilities as a board member of your bank and/or holding company are identical.

Federal Reserve System Board of Governors [FRB]
Proposed Board Effectiveness [BE] Guidance [August 3, 2017]

The Board invites comment on a proposal addressing supervisory expectations for boards of directors of bank and savings and loan holding companies and state member banks of all sizes.

The proposal would establish principles regarding effective boards of directors focused on the performance of a board's core responsibilities. The proposal would also better distinguish between the roles and responsibilities of an institution's board of directors and those of senior management.

The proposed BE guidance describes effective boards as those which:

[1] Set clear, aligned, and consistent direction regarding the firm's strategy and risk tolerance,
[2] Actively manage information flow and board discussions,
[3] Hold senior management accountable,
[4] Support the independence and stature of independent risk management and internal audit, and
[5] Maintain a capable board composition and governance structure.

#   #   #

Chapter Nine

Board Committee Organization

"The achievements of an organization are the results of the combined effort of each individual."

Vince Lombardi

Your board committees provide an efficient method to distribute your board's workload and responsibilities and provide an appropriate forum for more detailed discussion of specific topics [audit, compliance, risk, etc.] at the committee level.

Your committees need to have a specific charter that serves as the "job description" for each committee. The charter needs to be in writing and adopted by the full board.

Each committee chair needs to coordinate with a primary management contact to help organize committee agendas and distribute materials and take minutes.

Appropriate utilization of your board committees will permit summarized reports by your committee chairs to the full board on important matters and will help make your full board meetings more time efficient.

To effectively utilize board members' time, your board may want to consider limiting the number of board members assigned to each committee. For example, to distribute the workload, a ten-member board may consider electing three independent board members to each committee with most board members serving on two committees.

Director Independence

Extensions of credit by your bank to a director should not preclude a finding of director independence as long as the loans are [a] made in the ordinary course of business on substantially the same terms and conditions for comparable loans to unrelated persons; and [b] not on nonaccrual status, past due, restructured or potential problem loans.

Your board determines the "independence" of directors for this purpose. When there is any doubt about independence the director should be recused from any discussions that might be influenced by that relationship.

Executive Committee?

Your board may consider having an executive committee with authority to act between board meetings if necessary. However, such a committee should not need to meet frequently nor should a majority of board members be on the committee.

Your executive committee should not be structured as a super committee that creates a two-tier board and excludes other board members from important decisions.

Your other board members should be notified in the event this committee meets between meetings and any action should be reported and ratified, if appropriate, at the next regular board meeting.

Committee Charters

Your bank's committee charters are the "job description" for committee members and provide the basis for each committee's annual evaluation of their activities and performance.

Your committees' performance evaluations must be more than "check the box" on a questionnaire. This evaluation is more than reviewing charters and confirming every duty has been performed. Your committees also need to candidly consider the performance of each member and make certain their committee has the right number of qualified members to perform the assigned duties.

Private Sessions

Board committees should conduct a private session at the conclusion of each committee meeting with appropriate individuals such as the CEO, the internal and/or external auditors and chief credit officer. Such sessions provide a direct private forum for such officers to share any concerns or problems with members of your board committees.

If a significant issue is disclosed during such a private session, it is to be shared promptly by the committee chair with your Lead Director. The matter may then be discussed in private between the Lead Director and CEO and any action taken reported by the Lead Director and/or CEO to all board members during your next executive session.

#   #   #

Chapter Ten

Audit Committee

"You can observe a lot by just watching."

Yogi Berra

Audit committees have historically been burdened with increasing responsibilities for bank risk and compliance oversight. My experience indicates that more effective board governance and oversight is achieved by distributing part of this workload to separate board committees established for risk oversight and regulatory compliance.

Your audit committee already has a significant job in fulfilling its responsibilities related to monitoring your bank's financial and operating controls and the integrity of the bank's financial statements.

A regulatory & compliance committee, Chapter Thirteen, can be established to review all legal and regulatory requirements subject to board oversight and to monitor management's compliance procedures.

A risk committee, Chapter Fourteen, may be established to set risk policy "curbs" and look out the "windshield" to monitor changing trends to keep your bank "out of the ditch".

Assuming your bank adopts this committee structure then your audit committee charter and duties would describe your audit committee's remaining responsibilities.

> *The following charter and duties are not all-inclusive and are intended to serve as an example of the responsibilities and typical duties of an audit committee:*

Audit Committee Charter

Members of the committee shall be appointed by your board, each member shall meet the standards for an "Independent Non-Employee Director".

The members of the committee may designate a Chair by vote of the committee members, unless your board appoints the Chair.

The committee shall meet at least four times annually or more frequently as circumstances dictate.

Minutes of committee meetings shall be maintained and regularly submitted to the board. The committee may make appropriate recommendations to the board.

All members of the committee shall be able to read and understand fundamental financial statements and at least one member of the committee should have accounting or related financial management expertise. [Chapter Six]

Each member of the committee shall be and remain free of any relationship that could influence his or her judgment as a committee member.

The committee may retain and pay independent counsel, auditors, accountants or other professional advisors to the extent it deems necessary to carry out its duties.

The committee may conduct or authorize investigations into matters within the scope of its responsibilities.

Each member of the committee shall participate in appropriate educational programs.

The committee shall perform an annual self-evaluation of the committee's activities to assess its skills, competence, independence, and committee's performance of the duties required by its charter.

The committee shall annually review and update the committee's charter and present any recommended changes to the board for its approval.

Typical Duties: Audit Committee

Review the reliability and integrity of financial information and related disclosures provided to the shareholders, regulators and other external parties.

Review the qualifications and independence of the external and internal auditors.

Review the performance of the external and the internal auditors.

Review the adequacy of the systems of internal control, including compliance with the provisions of bank regulatory authorities.

Review work performed by other external and internal examination parties, such as credit quality examiners.

Conduct or authorize investigations into matters within the scope of its responsibilities.

Establish and maintain procedures for the receipt, retention and treatment of complaints received regarding accounting, internal accounting controls or auditing matters, including the confidential, anonymous submissions by employees of concerns regarding questionable accounting or auditing matters.

Determine the fees and terms of engagement of, oversee and, where appropriate, dismiss the public accounting firm to be used as the external auditor, and periodically evaluate its independence and effectiveness.

Annually evaluate the quality of the external auditor.

Confirm and assure the independence of the external auditor.

Hire, select or appoint the individual or organization responsible for internal audit.

Approve before use all external audit services and any non-audit services of the external auditor. Management shall not have authority to engage the external auditor for any services without prior approval of the committee.

Consider, in consultation with the external auditor and internal audit, the audit scope, procedures and plans recommended by the internal auditor and the external auditor.

Ascertain that the external auditor views the committee as its client and that the auditor will be available to the board at least annually.

Ask management, internal audit and the external auditor about significant risks and exposures and assess management's steps to minimize them.

Review the adequacy of the bank's internal controls, including computerized information system controls and security with the external auditor and internal audit.

Review any significant findings and recommendations made by the external auditor or internal auditing, together with management's responses to them.

Review the results of the annual assessment of internal controls and the testing performed by the bank's personnel and internal auditor, and the subsequent assessment and testing performed by the external auditor.

Shortly after the annual audit is completed, the committee will review the following:

> Review the annual financial statements and related footnotes with management and the external auditor.

> Review the external auditor's audit of and report on the financial statements.

> Review any serious difficulties or disputes the external auditor encountered with management during the course of the audit.

The committee will consider and review with management and internal audit:

> Review internal audit and loan review reports (whether internal or external) and related significant findings during the year and management's responses to them.

> Review any difficulties the internal auditor encountered while conducting audits, including any restrictions on the scope of their work or access to required information.

> Review and approve internal audit's budget and staffing.

Review and discuss with the external auditor and management the bank's interim financial reports.

Review with management, the external auditor, the internal auditor and bank counsel any certification provided by management related to the bank's financial statements

Review with management and the external auditor significant financial reporting issues and judgments made in connection with the preparation of the bank's financial statements

Review with management and the external auditor the effect of regulatory and accounting initiatives as well as off-balance sheet structures on the bank's financial statements.

Review policies and procedures covering officers' expense accounts and perquisites, including their use of corporate assets, and consider the results of any audit of those areas by the internal auditor or the external auditor.

Meet with the internal auditor, the external auditor, Chief Financial Officer, Chief Credit Officer and other members of management selected by the committee in separate executive sessions for private discussions.

#   #   #

Chapter Eleven

Compensation Committee

"The spirit of envy can destroy; it can never build."

Margaret Thatcher

Your compensation committee evaluates the performance and pay of your CEO. Shareholder expectations and regulatory requirements for the evaluation of the performance and pay of your chief executive officer and other members of your executive team continue to evolve.

The guiding principles for executive incentive compensation programs [both stock and cash] require that payments be linked to sustained performance over time. Your committee's most significant compensation challenge today is the determination of realistic performance expectations.

The current economic environment combined with higher regulatory capital requirements impacts performance benchmarks such as return on shareholder equity. Your committee's challenge is to focus on both the benchmarks used to measure performance and to determine the level of long-term performance that represents an acceptable target for incentive compensation payments.

Compensation consultants generally compare compensation plans to "peer groups". Peer performance information is available from many sources including the Uniform Bank Performance Report [UBPR]. However, your committee needs to consider that performance calculated for regulatory peer groups is just "average" not "superior" performance. Peer group data should only be used as a guide, and not a mathematical calculation to be followed without further analysis.

Management incentive plans and payouts need to be linked to your bank's performance expectations. If your bank is in a "turnaround" situation with a new CEO then a target linked to improving year-to-year results might well represent a reasonable performance plan. On the other hand, if your bank currently exceeds peer performance then higher relative performance targets are more likely appropriate.

Setting realistic long-term performance targets by your committee is a challenging job in today's economic and regulatory environment.

Comprehensive incentive compensation and training plans at all levels are also essential for internal risk management.

For example: Chartwell's assignments during the financial crisis uncovered incentive compensation plans that were established without an appropriate "check and balance".

One such plan had retained incentive payments for loan volume for an individual that had been promoted to Chief Credit Officer. The plan did not match this officer's new responsibilities and it continued to pay incentives for loan growth rather than credit quality. This bank got what it paid for; rapid loan growth, excessive risk, excessive losses and a regulatory order.

Any loan officer incentive plan based on volume requires a strong system of independent credit approval, including a potential veto by your credit officers to ensure that your loan officers can't ignore or overrule your credit policies.

> *The following charter and duties are not all-inclusive and are intended to serve as an example of the responsibilities and typical duties of a compensation committee:*

Compensation Committee Charter

Members of the committee shall be appointed by your board, each member shall meet the standards for an "Independent Non-Employee Director".

The members of the committee may designate a Chair by vote of the committee members, unless your board appoints the Chair.

The committee shall meet at least four times annually or more frequently as circumstances dictate.

Minutes of committee meetings shall be maintained and regularly submitted to the board. The committee may make appropriate recommendations to the board.

Each member of the committee shall be and remain free of any relationship that could influence his or her judgment as a committee member.

The committee may retain and pay independent counsel, auditors, accountants or other professional advisors to the extent it deems necessary to carry out its duties.

The committee may conduct or authorize investigations into matters within the scope of its responsibilities.

Each member of the committee shall participate in appropriate educational programs.

The committee shall perform an annual self-evaluation of the committee's activities to assess its skills, competence, independence, and committee's performance of the duties required by its charter.

The committee shall annually review and update the committee's charter and present any recommended changes to the board for its approval.

Typically Duties: Compensation Committee

Evaluate the relationship between the performance of the bank, the performance of the executive officers [as defined by the committee], and the bank's compensation policies in approving the executive officers' compensation.

Consider the CEO's performance in determining the CEO's annual base salary.

Determine and approve all compensation payable, including all incentive awards, to the CEO and approve the CEO's recommendations for the other executive officers.

Compensation information is available for other officer positions, not just the CEO, and it would be advisable to obtain peer compensation information for your other executive officers, such as the CFO, CCO and CLO.

Authorize the bank to enter into, and approve the terms of, any employment, separation, supplemental benefit or other compensation related agreements with any executive officer.

Approve the terms of any bonus or incentive compensation plans, including setting and determining compliance with performance objectives.

Approve all stock-based, profit sharing and all other awards paid to management [as defined by the committee] under the terms of the bank's management incentive plans.

Approve the payment and amount of any discretionary award paid to any member of management.

Approve the amount of any discretionary contribution to be made by the bank to its employee benefit plans.

Annually review the bank's policies on perquisites and the value of perquisites for executive officers and directors. No changes in perquisites for executive officers and directors shall be made without prior committee approval.

Monitor changes in stock ownership of executive officers and directors.

Annually evaluate total personnel costs and consider how

the bank's compensation policies and amounts paid compare to peer group banks.

Review director compensation, including comparisons to peer group banks, at least every other year and make recommendations as required to the board.

#   #   #

Chapter Twelve

Nominating & Governance Committee

"It is not often that [people] learn from the past, even rarer that they draw the correct conclusions from it."

Henry Kissinger

Does your bank have the right mix of board talent combined with the right management team to guide your institution in today's economic and regulatory environment?

A nominating & governance committee [Nom/Gov] typically has responsibility for reviewing board membership and succession, senior management succession and other matters related to bank governance.

Board Refreshment

"Board Refreshment" and "Diversity" are the current buzzwords for board member recruitment. The media focus on the addition of women and minorities tends to emphasize ratios and overlook the skills and perspective required of new board members.

Many boards today tend to look alike, duplicate skills and exhibit "mirror image" perspectives rather than represent the diverse range of skills and new perspectives needed to be effective.

Your committee's toughest challenge may not be adding new skills but replacing people, deciding when your board is best served by replacing an existing board member. Your board expects management to replace poor performers and fill each job by recruiting or promoting quality people. It's necessary for directors to take the same actions at the board level.

Some boards may decide to impose a mandatory retirement age for directors. While this has both good and bad attributes, it sometimes can make it easier to "ease out" a long-term board member who is no longer being effective.

Management Succession

It's a sad commentary on board leadership that many banks have no CEO succession plan. When carefully examined, the sale of many banks due to "regulatory burden" was actually due to limited management depth and no meaningful CEO succession planning.

Board Assessments

Many organizations, including the American Association of Bank Directors, offer a variety of tools for the internal evaluation of your board's performance. Utilizing a simple questionnaire that provides "feel good" results is a waste of time – worthwhile board evaluations are hard work. It's not easy to evaluate your board's performance or for you to pass judgment on the quality of other board members.

Board assessments provide your board with the opportunity to take early intervention when potential board governance or board membership issues develop.

> *The American Association of Bank Directors [AABD] recommends that bank boards retain a third-party every third year to conduct a confidential 360° assessment of board governance including [a] a self-assessment by each board member, [b] a group assessment of each board member and [c] an assessment of your board by executive management.*

Finally, take the time to look in the mirror and accurately evaluate your own performance. The increased regulatory burden has also increased your individual responsibilities. Are you doing your job?

Board Recruitment

The first source of potential candidates to join your board most likely starts with existing board members and your executive management team. Be aware that existing board members and the CEO tend to recommend people who "look and think" as they do. While useful as a "first pass", you must dig beyond such recommendations.

Remember, you are looking for specific talents to add to your board, not just filling a board seat with a nice neighbor or business associate.

It might be beneficial to widen your search by considering potential candidates at a business or professional firm that may fill your specific requirements.

A significant challenge for many community banks is identifying candidates that will qualify as "independent".

The ever-growing regulatory burden makes it increasingly difficult to recruit qualified board members. The AABD has published a report that identifies over 800 rules and regulations that impact bank board members [page 109]. Your regulatory responsibilities make it even more important that you have the right mix of people and skills on your bank's board.

Board Education

Every board member should have enough interest in learning more about some aspect of banking that they are willing to attend at least one educational session each year.

Educational meetings and online programs are offered by state and national banking associations, law firms, accounting firms, consulting firms, investment banking firms, bank regulators, banking publications, etc.

Bank directors have ample opportunity to participate in one

or more bank educational programs every year and your bank should pay for at least one such educational session.

> *The following charter and duties are not all-inclusive and are intended to serve as an example of the responsibilities and typical duties of a Nom/Gov committee:*

Nomination & Governance Committee Charter

Members of the committee shall be appointed by your board, each member shall meet the standards for an "Independent Non-Employee Director".

The members of the committee may designate a Chair by vote of the committee members, unless your board appoints the Chair.

Each member of the committee shall be and remain free of any relationship that could influence his or her judgment as a committee member.

The committee shall meet at least three times annually or more frequently as circumstances dictate.

Minutes of committee meetings shall be maintained and regularly submitted to the board. The committee may make appropriate recommendations to the board.

The committee may retain and pay independent counsel, auditors, accountants or other professional advisors to the extent it deems necessary to carry out its duties.

The committee may conduct or authorize investigations into matters within the scope of its responsibilities.

Each member of the committee shall participate in appropriate educational programs.

The committee shall perform an annual self-evaluation of the committee's activities and its performance of the duties required by its charter.

The committee shall annually review and update the committee's charter and present any recommended changes to the board for its approval.

Typical Duties: Nom/Gov Committee

Develop and recommend to the board, from time to time as it deems appropriate, corporate governance policies, review such policies as necessary and recommend any modifications.

Consider corporate governance issues that may arise from time to time and make recommendations to the board.

Annually review the composition of the board to determine whether additional members with different qualifications or areas of expertise are needed to further enhance the composition of the board.

Prepare a board skills matrix to evaluate, identify and review the qualifications of current board members and identify the skills that should be added to the board.

Recommend for approval of the board the slate of nominees for inclusion in the bank's proxy statement.

Recommend for approval by the board the proposed membership of board committees.

Consider any communication from bank shareholders, including board member recommendation, which is properly submitted.

Annually distribute a board assessment, board member assessment and board member self-assessment to all board members for review by the committee.

Retain an independent third party to conduct a board and

board member assessment every third year.

Annually review the performance of the board and individual board members before nominating them for re-election.

Annually review all board committees and recommend to the full board, as appropriate, changes in number, function or composition of committees.

Annually review and recommend for board approval a Related Party Transaction Policy.

Annually review and recommend for board approval a Board Member Expectations Policy for distribution and acceptance by all bank directors.

Recommend a Code of Conduct Policy for board approval and annually distribute to the board and management the bank's code of conduct policy.

Recommend an Insider Trading Policy relating the bank's securities [if appropriate] for board approval.

Review the bank's directors' and officers' liability insurance coverage at each renewal.

Annually review and make recommendations to the board with respect to management succession.

Confer, as appropriate, with outside legal counsel on matters of corporate governance.

#   #   #

Chapter Thirteen

Regulatory & Compliance Committee

*"If you have ten thousand regulations
you destroy all respect for the law."*

Winston Churchill

Compliance with bank regulations is a given – you have no choice. Many bank regulations state that "management and the board shall" comply with the regulation with little or no distinction between the roles of management and the board.

Bank regulators have made it clear that bank directors are ultimately responsible if management fails to comply with bank regulations.

Bank regulators refusal to clearly separate the roles of day-to-day management and independent director oversight has been a major contributor to the existing 800+ rules and regulations identified by the AABD in the "Bank Director Regulatory Burden Report". [page 109]

One solution for coping with your board's growing compliance oversight responsibilities is to reexamine your board's committee structure and redistribute the workload.

Would your board benefit from a board regulatory & compliance committee to focus on regulatory compliance?

The establishment of a board regulatory & compliance committee could permit your over-burdened audit committee to refocus on financial controls and audits. Would such a committee structure help your board focus more of its meeting time on your customers, current performance and future strategy?

Regulatory & Compliance Committee Charter

Members of the committee shall be appointed by your board and may include the Chief Executive Officer.

Each member of the committee, other than the Chief Executive Officer, shall be an "Independent Non-Employee Director".

The members of the committee may designate a Chair by vote of the committee members, unless your board appoints the Chair.

The committee shall meet at least four times annually or more frequently as circumstances dictate.

Each member of the committee shall be and remain free of any relationship that could influence his or her judgment as a committee member.

Minutes of committee meetings shall be maintained and regularly submitted to the board.

The committee may retain and pay independent counsel, auditors, accountants or other professional advisors to the extent it deems necessary to perform its duties.

The committee may conduct or authorize investigations into matters within the scope of its responsibilities.

The committee may obtain advice and assistance from any bank officer or employee and shall have direct access to such officer or employee, as it deems necessary.

The committee may request that any bank officer or employee or outside advisor be present at its meetings.

Each member of the committee shall participate in appropriate educational programs.

The committee shall perform an annual self-evaluation of the committee's activities and performance of the duties required by its charter.

The committee shall perform an annual review of the committee's charter and present any recommended changes to the board for its approval.

Typical Duties: Regulatory & Compliance Committee

Consider bank regulatory issues that may arise from time to time and make policy recommendations to the board.

Assess the bank's regulatory compliance obligations and associated compliance risks.

Annually review the bank's regulatory and compliance policies and recommend approval with any changes to the board.

Oversee the bank's compliance management system and management's related processes and procedures.

Review management reports that monitor the bank's compliance systems, processes and transactions.

Investigate alleged compliance misconduct and, if required, recommend corrective action to management and enforce a compliance culture.

> *Some institutions set up a 'tip line' or 'hot line' and encourage any employee to anonymously raise issues of perceived misconduct. There are also third party contractors who may be used to set up such a reporting tool and then to bring the information to your committee.*

Review the effectiveness of the bank's compliance

management system and related processes and procedures.

Oversee the bank's participation in any governmental investigation related to regulatory compliance.

Receive reports prepared by the bank's Chief Compliance Officer regarding compliance management systems including any significant compliance investigations.

Receive audit reports from the bank's internal auditor regarding all regulatory compliance audits.

Review and make recommendations to the board, during meetings or in executive session, as appropriate, with respect to bank regulatory compliance matters.

Confer, as appropriate, with outside legal counsel on corporate and bank regulatory matters.

Take such further actions or provide such further advice as the full board may from time to time delegate to the committee.

#   #   #

Chapter Fourteen

Risk Committee

*"If you can't explain it simply,
you don't understand it well enough."*

Albert Einstein

Is your board prepared to discuss risk oversight with your bank's regulators in your next exit meeting? What will bank regulators expect your board to be doing in your role of risk oversight?

Your bank's strategic plan is the starting point for defining the level of risk [risk appetite] that your management and the board are willing to undertake to achieve your financial objectives. For example, your plan's definitions of target loan types, credit criteria, size limits, geographic exposure and concentration limits will help set your bank's credit risk parameters.

Banking is the art of managing risk, not eliminating risk. People at all levels of your organization engage in risky activity every day – cashing checks, taking deposits, making and renewing loans, buying securities, processing customer information, etc.

An organizational structure that provides your bank with independent credit and risk management personnel combined with an independent internal audit function will help provide an appropriate "trust but verify" structure that helps prevent both management and board surprises.

Talent management, including compliance training and appropriate compensation plans at all levels, is also essential for internal risk management. In any event, an appropriate tone at the top is critical to establishing a sound risk management culture.

Many banks have established board risk committees. The role for such a committee must be carefully integrated with the role of the full board and other committees such as audit. If not well structured just adding a new risk committee within your existing board committee structure may be counterproductive.

The typical risk committee approves policy limits and provides oversight for credit policy, loan concentrations, interest rate risk, reputational risk and for operational and technology risks. The work related to credit and interest rate risk oversight is an appropriate assignment for a board risk committee and provides an opportunity to replace existing board committees such as loan and investment.

Your committee's review and evaluation of risk reports is an ever-evolving process. The objective of this chapter is to provide you with guidance on how to approach your duties as a director – not teach you to evaluate specific reports.

Understanding management reports and presentations is obviously important. You should undertake any specific educational steps you think are necessary to comprehend the risk your management team is presenting.

The distinction of duties between a risk committee, audit committee and regulatory compliance committee can be described as the following:

> A risk committee's job is approving and monitoring risk polices – looking out the windshield and providing guidance to keep your bank out of the ditch.

> The role of an audit committee is to confirm that management is operating within the risk policies and limits established by the risk committee.

> The role of a regulatory & compliance committee is to confirm that bank operations comply with bank laws and regulations.

A risk committee is complementary, not an overlap with audit and regulatory compliance committee responsibilities. Some degree of shared committee membership may help avoid overlap and prevent gaps and committee chairs should compare committee activities at least once a year to avoid duplication and prevent gaps in coverage.

Designing an effective risk governance framework is a difficult task for both management and the board of directors to implement. Linking the various elements together while maintaining an appropriate separation of duties and independence is an especially difficult task for community banks with limited personnel and financial resources.

Your committee may decide to adopt a formal risk appetite framework [RAF]. Such an RAF would describe your bank's risk philosophy and state risk appetite, risk profile, risk capacity and risk limits with reference to all bank risk policies. All risk policy limits must be considered as a whole to understand your bank's consolidated risk profile.

Many consulting firms have expanded their services to include enterprise risk management [ERM]. If your committee decides to seek outside guidance, it is important for your committee to maintain perspective and not just adopt a cookie-cutter ERM program designed to enhance fee income for a consulting firm.

Organizationally, the typical bank measures and manages risk according to three main risk categories: credit risk, market risk [including interest rate and liquidity risk], and operating risk [including compliance risk].

> Credit and loan risk is typically the management responsibility of a Chief Credit Officer.

> Capital and market risk [interest rate & liquidity] is typically the management responsibility of the Chief Financial Officer.

> Operating and compliance risk is typically the management responsibility of the Chief Operations Officer

Each of these individuals should make regular status reports to your risk committee.

> The following charter and duties are not all-inclusive and are intended to serve as an example of the responsibilities and typical duties of a risk committee:

Risk Committee Charter

Members of the committee shall be appointed by your board and may include the Chief Executive Officer.

Each member of the committee, other than the Chief Executive Officer, shall be an "Independent Non-Employee Director".

The members of the committee may designate a Chair by vote of the committee members, unless your board appoints the Chair.

The committee shall meet at least eight times annually or more frequently as circumstances dictate.

Minutes of committee meetings shall be maintained and regularly submitted to the board. The committee may make appropriate recommendations to the board.

Each member of the committee shall be and remain free of any relationship that could influence his or her judgment as a committee member.

The committee may retain and pay independent counsel, auditors, accountants or other professional advisors necessary to perform its duties.

The committee may conduct or authorize investigations into matters within the scope of its responsibilities.

The committee may obtain advice and assistance from any bank officer or employee and shall have direct access to such officer or employee, as it deems necessary.

The committee may request that any bank officer or employee or outside advisor be present at its meetings.

Each member of the committee shall participate in appropriate educational programs.

The committee shall perform an annual self-evaluation of the committee's activities and performance of the duties required by its charter.

The committee shall perform an annual review of the committee's charter and present any recommended changes to the board for its approval.

Typical Duties: Risk Committee

Management is responsible for maintaining operational controls and procedures designed to provide reasonable assurance of compliance with credit and other risk policies approved by the committee.

The audit committee is responsible for oversight of management's compliance with the bank's credit risk policy, market risk policy and compliance with the bank's operating risk policies.

The committee is to provide an open avenue of communication regarding credit, market and operating risk management among management and the board.

The committee may request any officer or employee of the bank, the bank's outside counsel, external auditor or internal auditor to attend a meeting of the committee or to meet with any members of, or consultants to, the committee. The committee is authorized to request and receive all pertinent information from management.

The committee is responsible for approval and oversight of credit and risk management policies as recommended to the committee by management.

Credit Risk Policy

The committee shall be responsible for reviewing and approving a written credit policy for the bank, to be prepared and periodically updated by Chief Credit Officer.

The Chief Credit Officer may not be appointed, replaced, reassigned or dismissed without the approval of the committee.

The credit policy will govern the credit risk of all assets including non-loan credit risk such as investment portfolio risk, derivative counter parties, lessee risk, etc.

The committee shall review policies and review limits for each credit category at least annually or as conditions dictate. The objective of the credit policy shall be to ensure the credit quality of the bank's portfolios and to maintain profitability of the bank.

The credit policy shall establish certain credit quality ratios to monitor credit quality and related ratios.

The committee shall establish credit quality "trigger ratios" that require management to prepare an action plan for corrective action. The Chief Credit Officer is responsible for notifying the committee whenever a credit quality ratio "triggers" the requirement for corrective action. An action plan is to be prepared and presented to the committee any time any ratio exceeds such a trigger ratio.

The committee shall review the credit policy not less than annually to confirm that the policy conforms to applicable laws and regulations. The credit policy shall include, without limitation, lending policies for all the divisions of the company.

The committee shall approve the bank's in-house lending limits. The credit policy shall provide that all loans will require the approval of the appropriate loan officers, the Chief Credit Officer and a management credit committee.

The credit policy shall also establish thresholds for loan relationships that require disclosure for informational purposes to the committee.

> *The American Association of Bank Directors [AABD] recommends that bank board members not approve individual loans [other than loans subject to Regulation O or involving certain insider conflicts].*
>
> *This AABD recommendation and related communication with the FDIC is included in the AABD report: "FDIC Director Suits: Lessons Learned". [page 109]*

The committee shall, upon consultation with management, approve portfolio guidelines and limitations for new and existing loan products and services.

The Chief Credit Officer shall provide the committee with periodic reports of loans, loan activity and loan portfolio information.

The audit committee, in consultation with the committee, may retain the services of an external examination firm to perform an independent credit review. The external examination firm shall report credit review findings to both the risk committee and the audit committee.

The risk committee and audit committee shall have the opportunity to meet at any time with the external examination firm without including any of the members or representatives of management.

The committee shall evaluate, not less than annually, the effectiveness of the independent credit review provided by an external examination firm and report such evaluation to the audit committee.

The Chief Financial Officer shall periodically [not less than quarterly] provide the committee with an analysis and confirmation that the bank is maintaining a sufficient allowance for loan and lease losses ["ALLL"].

Asset/Liability & Liquidity Risk Policy

The committee shall be responsible for reviewing and approving a written Asset/Liability Policy ["ALCO"], to be prepared and periodically [not less than annually] updated by the Chief Financial Officer.

Asset/Liability and liquidity management is a management responsibility. The ALCO Policy shall establish a management asset/liability committee and the Chief Financial Officer shall provide the risk committee with monthly financial reports to ensure compliance with the ALCO Policy.

The ALCO Policy will govern interest rate risk and liquidly policy for the bank. The primary objective of the ALCO Policy is to manage market risk and to ensure profitability of the bank.

The ALCO Policy shall require the utilization of a simulation model to project the impact of changing interest rates on bank earnings, liquidity and capital. The committee shall approve policy limits for interest rate and liquidity risk.

The financial projections calculated by the simulation model shall be reviewed by the committee no less than quarterly.

Operating Risk Policy

Management shall establish an operating risk committee to be chaired by the bank's chief operations officer to review, evaluate and establish Operating Risk Policy for the bank.

A management operating risk committee is typically structured to recommend operating policies and provide management oversight of technology risk, deposit operations risk, loan operations risk, trust operations risk and any other activity that presents an operating risk.

The Chief Operations Officer shall present an operating risk policy to the committee for its review and approval.

The Chief Operations Officer shall provide periodic reports to the committee and shall report any violations of operating risk policy to the committee.

The risk committee may engage third parties to test specific areas of operating risk from time to time.

Reputational Risk

FDIC: "Reputational risk is of utmost importance to financial institutions because of the central role public confidence plays in their success and the bank's liquidity".

Any number of activities can "go wrong" and potentially contribute to reputational risk. The advent of the Internet and social media for the distribution of "news", accurate or not, can escalate a potential reputational risk significantly.

It is important for management to monitor any reports and rumors that could potentially impact the bank's reputation.

Bank directors also need to be sensitive to internal and external events that could impact your banks reputation.

The CEO shall be responsible for providing the committee with an action plan in the event external or internal circumstances require a public response to actual or perceived reputational risk.

#   #   #

Remember Einstein's words when you ask questions and request information from management.

Keep asking questions until you understand management's explanation. Your officers need to understand risk control well enough to make it understandable to you.

*"If you can't explain it simply,
you don't understand it well enough."*

Albert Einstein

Chapter Fifteen

Strategy & Planning

*"If you don't know where you are going
you might wind up someplace else."*

Yogi Berra

Why a Strategic Plan?

Navigating a small sailboat to a distant destination is my analogy for strategic planning. For example, sailing your boat from Florida to Bermuda is a voyage of opportunity, uncertainty and danger.

First: You determine the destination for the voyage – in this example your goal is to safely sail to Bermuda.

Strategic planning for your bank requires your CEO and board to establish clear understandable strategic goals; earnings growth, profitability, asset growth, market share, etc....

It is essential to focus on a few key goals that everyone can keep top of mind. Your goals are too complex if a manager is unable to explain the goals to a staff member without notes.

Second: You must have a qualified and experienced crew that can work together as a team to safely complete the voyage to Bermuda. Crewmembers need the knowledge to stand watch alone, stay on course, trim sails for efficient speed and call on their experience to ask for help when required.

The same is true for your bank; you need qualified and experienced management in every position who can work together as a team to achieve your common goal.

Third: Preparing your sailboat for the voyage is essential. You must make certain that all the equipment [sailing, safety, etc] is the correct quality for an offshore voyage where weather and sea conditions can be very rough.

To compete, your bank must offer quality competitive products and services that your customers want and use.

A classic business school case study describes a firm testing its marketing strategy for a new dog food with dog owners and pet stores. Based on this research the marketing programs and advertising were completed and the product was introduced.

Actual sales were a disaster – the dogs didn't like it!

**"However beautiful the strategy,
you should occasionally look at the results."**

Winston Churchill

Fourth: You plot the planned course to sail from Florida to Bermuda. Multiple alternatives exist; sail the Northwest Passage through the Bahamas, follow the gulfstream north along the coast, etc. Your planned course must also avoid hazards such as shallow water and coral reefs.

Determining your planned course [strategy] depends on the long-term weather forecast. For example, a north wind at the start of your voyage would make the gulfstream dangerous, but provide a safe passage through the Bahamas.

This step is equivalent to bank management recommending a competitive strategy to achieve your bank's strategic goals, as your bank must navigate through changing, competitive and economic conditions.

Fifth: Long-term weather forecasts are not dependable and wind and sea conditions will change during your voyage.

You will need to make tactical course adjustments; your course may change to accommodate a wind or current shift but the goal of safely sailing to Bermuda remains the same.

Economic forecasts are not dependable and competitive conditions are subject to change. Therefore, your bank's management may also be required to adjust tactics to meeting changing economic and competitive conditions but the goals [earnings growth, etc.] remain the same.

Sixth: Your voyage to Bermuda is complete when your sailboat safely enters the harbor, but where do you go from Bermuda? Sailing is a never-ending voyage so long as your sailboat is sound and your crew is ready.

The same is true for your bank - strategic planning is a never-ending process designed to keep the bank consistently competitive with the right management team in place. As a result, your board should certainly consider holding a special meeting devoted only to strategic planning at least once a year.

Finally, some banks reach a point that the sale of the bank appears to be the best strategic alternative for its shareholders. But even in this case a bank that has been managed well will achieve the best price for its shareholders.

Strategy & Risk Oversight

Balancing your bank's long-term growth strategy with appropriate risk oversight is a significant challenge for your bank's directors. You need to address risk oversight when management presents their long-term plans and annual budget to your board for approval.

Developing a realistic growth strategy in today's slow growth economic environment is a tough challenge for the management of every financial institution. Avoiding the temptation to take excessive risk to enhance future earnings is a significant challenge. However, your bank's business is managing risk, not avoiding all risks. So how does your board know when management has crossed your "risk" line?

Your board's risk policy and oversight [Chapter Fourteen] must be tailored to match your bank's strategy and actual operations.

The key to profitable growth is a realistic strategy for offering competitive banking services in your bank's markets. The dramatic changes underway in how bank customers access financial services presents a growing technological, marketing and competitive challenge.

Your board should make certain that management's strategic plan presents you with a candid view of your banks competitive strengths and weaknesses in your bank's markets. Make certain that management's plan specifically addresses existing and proposed products and services your bank may offer. Acknowledge that banking is mostly a commodity business and loan and deposit offerings are essentially the same at all institutions.

Marketing strategy and staff training are essential to providing any competitive advantage within a commodity business. Bank managements frequently claim that "our people are our most important competitive advantage" - but just what is your management team doing to attract, retain and train the most competitive staff in today's rapidly changing marketplace?

Low pricing is not a strategy; it's a weakness that will damage long-term profitability. How does your management plan to grow and maintain appropriate margins?

Lowering credit quality standards to keep or "steal" business from a competitor is not a strategy; it's a weakness that can lead to excessive loan losses. We all know how "subprime" lending worked out in the last decade.

Research indicates the most efficient firms in any commodity business, including banking, are typically the most profitable firms. Make certain that any costs designated as "investing in the future" have a real strategic purpose. Cost cutting is not a long-term growth strategy but maintaining efficient operations is essential to your bank's long-term profitability.

Prior to your board approval of management's budget and strategic plan, it's important to undertake a risk assessment to identify those areas that require policy discussions and detailed board oversight. For example:

> *Does the plan require a significant increase in an existing or new loan category?*

> *Does projected loan growth create a concentration or pricing risk?*

> *Does your bank have the appropriate credit, technology and operational systems to manage the projected growth?*

> *Does the plan project entering a new business?*

> *How does management plan to hire or train staff to manage the new business?*

> *Will the bank have the appropriate technology and operational systems to insure all products and services meet all regulatory compliance requirements?*

> *Does the plan anticipate entering new markets and expanding its geographic footprint?*

> *Why has management selected specific markets and what competitive advantage will the bank have following entry?*

> *Do existing or proposed incentive compensation plans encourage excessive risk?*

Just answering these and other questions during the budget and strategic planning discussion is not enough. The board must also establish an effective way to monitor results and management's future compliance with risk policy.

Once your board has approved management's strategic plan, the job of your risk committee is to look out the "windshield" to monitor operating trends and establish policy "curbs" to keep your bank "out of the ditch".

#   #   #

The following page is an outline of key topics utilized by Chartwell Capital to initiate strategic planning discussions with bank management. As a board member, you should make certain that your management addresses each of these elements or questions in your bank's strategic plan.

CHARTWELL CAPITAL LTD
Strategic Planning Outline

The following outline provides a working model for discussion, analysis and development of your bank's strategic plan.

Make certain every element of your bank's strategy fits together into a plan that works as a whole.

Shareholder Expectations?	Geographic Marketplace?
➢ Earnings [EPS] Growth ➢ Dividend Expectations ➢ Stock Price & Liquidity	➢ Demographics & Growth ➢ Potential Customers ➢ Competition
People Management?	**Asset Generation?**
➢ Existing Skills & Talent ➢ Additional Requirements ➢ Compensation Plans	➢ Loan Products & Pricing ➢ Portfolio Mix & Growth ➢ New Products or Acquisitions
Capital Management?	**Funding Requirements?**
➢ Regulatory Capital ➢ Dividend Policy ➢ Equity & Alternatives	➢ Deposit Mix & Growth ➢ Borrowings & Pricing ➢ Internal or Acquisitions
Fee Income Generation?	**Operating Efficiency?**
➢ Grow Existing Services ➢ New Services or Acquisitions ➢ Price, Margins & Growth	➢ Headcount Control ➢ Productivity Enhancement ➢ Divest Non-Core Business
Risk Management?	**Regulatory Considerations?**
➢ Credit Risk ➢ Interest Rates & Liquidity ➢ Operating & Compliance Risk	➢ Bank Regulations ➢ Employment, etc. ➢ Audit & Accounting

Your strategic plan is the internal roadmap for reaching your bank's long-term objectives. Management's annual operating plan or budget must then address the short-term actions management must accomplish in order to reach your long-term performance objectives.

It's essential that your bank's board and management reach agreement on realistic strategic performance objectives. This outline represents only a starting point for discussion and the development of your bank's strategic plan.

Chapter Sixteen

Bank M&A: Buy, Sell or Hold?

"The future ain't what it used to be."

Yogi Berra

Recent bank merger and acquisition [M&A] activity has been attributed to a variety of factors: low interest rates; declining margins; modest loan demand [at best]; increased competition from larger banks; and most important, increased regulatory requirements and costs. It's been especially easy to paint a gloomy picture for community banking.

Politicians and bank regulators have stressed the importance of community banking to local communities. However, many bankers question the sincerity of such public statements given the increased regulatory cost and compliance risk of doing business as a community bank. The reluctance of the FDIC to approve new charters following the financial crisis also brings into question its commitment to community banking.

Increased regulatory expectations combined with today's economic climate are forcing many banks to re-evaluate their business plans and performance expectations. Strategic discussions at many community banks have shifted from growth to finding an exit strategy and individual directors are questioning the wisdom of their continued bank board service.

Investment bankers are now extending dinner invitations to community bank executives. A few years ago these same investment bankers would not have returned a phone call from a community banker.

Successful strategic buyers want to acquire high quality banks in markets that offer the opportunity for future growth. However, acquirors must exercise pricing discipline if they are to achieve future profitability expectations. In addition, post-acquisition studies indicate that many bank combinations only increase size [and CEO compensation] but do not enhance shareholder value.

It's also essential that sellers conduct detailed due-diligence with qualified financial and legal advisors. Potential sellers must carefully evaluate the potential long-term value of any shares to be received in a proposed transaction. Beware of a deal that's "too good to be true".

For example, several years ago, Chartwell Capital successfully advised a client to reject a hostile acquisition exchange offer of the proposed acquiring bank's stock "valued" at $9.00/share at a time when the target's stock was $4.50/share. Two years later those $9.00 shares were worth less than a $1.00/share and the target's stock price had increased to over $9.00/share by remaining an independent bank.

Finally, it's very difficult, if not impossible, to make the numbers work for most potential M&A transactions between community banks of similar size.

A number of community banks with a desire to sell may have no logical buyer and be "orphans" with no choice but to enhance future value as an independent bank.

Planning to sell is not a plan!

Today's regulatory environment may be tossing "sand in the gears" but your bank still serves as the oil in the economic engine of your community.

Therefore, the objective for your board and executive management should be to "manage your institution as if you will own it forever" and focus on those actions you can take to serve your customers, prosper with your community and enhance shareholder value.

Community bankers have successfully identified survival and growth strategies following past recessions [1973-74, 1979-81, 1989-91 and 2007-09]. Well-managed banks emerged stronger after each of these troubled periods.

It really makes no difference if you want to buy, sell or remain independent. By "managing your bank as if you will own it forever" you will build a solid institution for the long term.

Well-managed community banks still serve an important role. Community banks can and do offer more personalized service than the large regional or national banks.

Technology provided by quality service providers helps level the playing field for community banks. Community banks can better manage their regulatory and compliance burden if they target products and services to their community and don't attempt to be all things to all people.

As a bank director, you and your management team have an obligation to your bank's shareholders to build a solid institution and enhance shareholder value. It won't be easy as an independent bank in today's environment but you may have no choice.

#   #   #

Chapter Seventeen

Kick the Can . . . or Time to Go?

*"Only God, who is immortal,
has no need of succession."*

Lactantius

As discussed in Chapter Twelve, your board must address board leadership, board size, required skill sets, board member performance and succession planning. Matching needed skill sets with your limited number of board seats is a tough job.

It is understandably difficult for your board to confront a fellow board member who is not fully contributing to your board's responsibilities. It is equally difficult for a board member to recognize when it is time to depart. It's easier for everyone to "kick the can down the road."

Some boards use term limits or age limits as a mechanism to force rotation of board members. However, such programs impact both "quality" directors and "problem" directors and most likely permit the board to avoid addressing a need for change by "kicking the can" until the "problem" member hits the term/age limit.

Nonprofit boards frequently honor and thank departing board members for their service with a wall plaque or other memento as they exit the board. Getting "plaqued" is a gracious way many nonprofits give board members an honorable exit and rotate board members.

So, do you still bring the right skills and work ethic to your bank's board or is it time for you get "plaqued"?

"It ain't over till it's over."
Yogi Berra

About the Author

Charles J Thayer is Chairman of Chartwell Capital Ltd., a firm specializing in financial and governance advisory services to board members and executive management of banks, corporations and institutional investors.

He is Chairman Emeritus of the American Association of Bank Directors [AABD] and served as Chairman from 2007 until 2013. The AABD is the national non-profit organization dedicated to serving the information, education and advocacy needs of financial institution directors.

Thayer served on the board of directors of MainSource Financial Group [NASDAQ] from June 2011 until May 2017, serving as Lead Director in 2016. MainSource is a $4.5 billion banking institution with locations in Indiana, Illinois, Ohio and Kentucky.

He was designated a Board Leadership Fellow by the National Association of Corporate Directors [NACD] in 2016. Thayer served as Program Chair for the NACD-AABD Bank Directors Workshop from 2006 to 2015 and he has served on the faculty for the NACD's Masters Class.

Thayer served on the board of trustees of the national Cystic Fibrosis Foundation for 37 years, from 1980 until May 2017. He served as Chairman of the foundation's investment committee from 1993 to 2011 and as Chairman of Cystic Fibrosis Services, Inc., the foundation's national mail order pharmacy, from 1994 to 2004.

He served on the board of the Louisville Development Bancorp [LDB] from 1997 until 2013. LDB's shareholders include Kentucky's major banks and corporations and LDB's banking subsidiary [Metro Bank] is dedicated to job creation and home ownership in the Louisville metro area.

He served on the boards of Republic Bancshares [NASDAQ] and Republic Bank, one of Florida's largest independent commercial banks, from 1999 until Republic was acquired by BB&T Corporation in 2004. Thayer served on the board of BB&T Bank [Florida] until July 2006.

CogenAmerica [NASDAQ], an independent power producer headquartered in Minneapolis, Minnesota, elected Thayer to its board of directors in April 1996. He served as a member of the Independent Directors Committee [IDC] until CogenAmerica's acquisition by Calpine Corporation in December 1999. The IDC was given full control of the acquisition process.

Thayer served on the board of directors of Sunbeam Corporation [NYSE] from 1990 until 1997. In January 1993 he was elected Chairman & CEO of Sunbeam, providing interim management until the election of a new CEO in August 1993.

Thayer had a twenty-year career in commercial banking prior to organizing Chartwell Capital in 1990. As Executive Vice President of PNC Financial [NYSE], Pittsburgh, he had management responsibility for finance, merger and acquisitions, investor relations, strategic planning, and he served as Chairman of PNC Securities Corp, PNC's capital markets subsidiary.

Prior to its acquisition by PNC in 1986, Thayer served as Executive Vice President and Chief Financial Officer of Citizens Fidelity [NASDAQ], Kentucky's largest banking institution.

Thayer is the author of "*It Is What It Is*" the book describing the recapitalization of AmericanWest Bank in 2010, and "*Credit Check*" a collection of stories describing the value of mentors. He has written numerous articles for a variety of banking publications and has been a frequent speaker at banking and corporate governance programs.

Previous Books

Charles J Thayer

2016 *"Credit Check"*
Giving Credit Where Credit Is Due

2010 *"It Is What It Is"*
Saving AmericanWest Bank

1986 *"The Bank Directors Handbook"*; 2nd Edition
Chapter: Asset/Liability Management

1983 *"Bankers Desk Reference"*
Warren, Gorham & Lamont
Chapter: The Financial Futures Market

1981 *"The Bank Directors Handbook"*; 1st Edition*
Chapter: Asset/Liability Management

Available at

American Association of Bank Directors

www.AABD.org

The American Association of Bank Directors [AABD] provides information, educational and advocacy for bank directors. My role as Chairman of the AABD [2007-2013] provided me with unique insight on the challenges faced by bank directors during and after the 2007-09 financial crisis.

The AABD was founded in 1989 in the midst of the S&L crisis and the AABD is the only banking trade association in the United States which exclusively serves individual directors rather than their financial institutions.

Additional educational information at: www.AABD.org

Special Reports Published by AABD

*2016   Practical Handbook on Fair Lending for
Bank Directors and Executive Officers*

2014   AABD's Bank Director Regulatory Burden Report

*2013   Bank Director Standards of Care and Protections:
A Fifty-State Survey*

2012   FDIC Director Suits - Lessons Learned

Available at

Acknowledgements

An undertaking such as this book is not done alone and I thank my friend, David Fannin, and my sister Linda for their help in reviewing my work. I also thank David Baris, AABD President, for the guidance he provided to me in my role as AABD Chairman during the 2007-09 financial crisis.

My professional career has required family and friends willing to endure my frequent travel and commitment to work. This is a condition that has been tolerated by my family and friends over the past fifty-years and I thank each of you and especially my wife, Molly, for your understanding.

Disclaimer

The views, opinions and suggestions expressed are mine and mine alone and do not necessarily reflect the policy of any banking association or bank regulator.

The information and guidance provided is intended to supplement information provided to you or your bank by your personal attorney, your bank's law firm and bank regulators. I am not an attorney and you should seek any legal or regulatory advice from your personal attorney or the bank's law firm.

Finally, there is no single "right" approach for all bank boards and others providing governance advice to bank directors could recommend other alternatives. There is no right "cookbook" for bank board governance and your board must determine its own "recipe" for success.

Charles J Thayer

Made in the USA
Middletown, DE
05 September 2017